MEMORY LANE
AYLESBURY
INTO THE SEVENTIES

Photographs from the archives of **The Bucks Herald** **Advertiser** BUCKS

MEMORY LANE
AYLESBURY
INTO THE SEVENTIES

breedon **books**
PUBLISHING

First published in Great Britain in 2002 by
The Breedon Books Publishing Company Limited
Breedon House, 3 The Parker Centre,
Derby, DE21 4SZ.

ISBN 1 85983 339 X

Printed and bound by Butler & Tanner, Frome,
Somerset, England.

Cover printing by Lawrence-Allen Colour Printers,
Weston-super-Mare, Somerset, England.

CONTENTS

INTRODUCTION

THE introduction to our first book – *Memory Lane Aylesbury: The Post War Years* – ended by saying that much had happened in Aylesbury and The Vale since the photographs included in the book were taken. 'But that is another story…' we said.

Here, in the following pages, readers have the chance to learn more about the recent past of the area and its people as we take another fond look back through the archives of *The Bucks Herald* and its sister paper *The Bucks Advertiser*.

This time it is a trip down memory lane Into The Seventies.

Such was the response to the first volume that it was decided not to wait too long before producing another. Perhaps its success is best summed up by the many wonderful stories that have been told since *Memory Lane Aylesbury: The Post War Years*, first appeared on bookshop shelves.

One such happened within hours of publication when, in the centre of the town, an elderly gentleman approached one of those responsible for carrying out the research and, with tears in his eyes, said simply: 'Thank you'.

In the book, he explained, there was a photograph of a street party held in Aylesbury to celebrate the Queen's Coronation which showed his late wife and his daughter who, at the time, was a babe-in-arms.

'We had the picture once but, as so often happens over the years, it was lost. When my wife died I went looking for it as it was the only picture I had of her around that time in our lives. I couldn't find it and thought I would never see it again. I just can't believe it,' he said.

Similar heartwarming stories have been told, not only by those still living locally but also many who have moved to other parts of the country and also abroad, including to Australia, America and Canada.

Often they received a copy of the book as a present and on its pages, and among more than 300 photographs, discovered family, friends… and even themselves!

There are so many stories that could be told as our chief photographer Barry Keen can testify.

He posted a copy to his brother, now living in Australia, pointing out in particular the photograph of a bus which had turned on to its side after skidding on an icy road in 1947, a bus on which their father had been a passenger. And what followed was, as he put it, 'a chance in a million'.

His brother showed our book to a friend who had also emigrated from this area many years ago, only to discover that his father had been the driver of the bus, something neither of them knew before and might never have known had it not been for that single photograph.

Both newspapers have been a part of the local community since the md-1800s and the use of nostalgia pictures has, for a long time, been a regular weekly feature in *The Bucks Herald*.

These often produce a similar response to that seen with the publication of our first book, reminding people of the way things once were and, in many cases, putting people back in touch, sometimes after many years.

We are confident this will be repeated with this latest volume.

While there is no way any book can paint a truly comprehensive picture of life as it was, it can provide a revealing glimpse of the town and district and, most importantly, the people.

We hope you enjoy it!

David Truen

To purchase copies of
photographs in this book
please contact:

The Bucks Herald and Advertiser,
2-4 Exchange Street, Aylesbury,
Bucks, HP20 1UJ.
Phone: 01296 318300.

A Right Royal Do

No prizes for guessing what is going on here, not when you know that the year is 1977. This was the scene at a street party held at Bedgrove, Aylesbury – just one of hundreds organised around the area – to celebrate the Queen's Silver Jubilee in June of that year.

They were flag waving like fury at this Jubilee street party held in Lancaster Road, Aylesbury.

Our photographer caught these residents of Elmhurst, Aylesbury, just about to tuck in to their Silver Jubilee street party feast in June 1977.

A special celebration cake was the centrepiece for this Jubilee party organised at Southcourt, Aylesbury in 1977.

They might have had to wrap up well for their Jubilee street party, but that didn't seem to bother these residents of Cannock Road, Aylesbury.

A children's fancy dress competition was all part of the fun for these youngsters of Hawthorn Close, Aylesbury, before they sat down to their special Jubilee feast – waited on by, who else, their parents and other residents of the street.

This Silver Jubilee party was held at Kinson Green, Aylesbury.

The Union Flag was flying high but not as high as the spirits of those taking part in a Jubilee street party at Hanover Close, Aylesbury in 1977.

It was a chance for everyone to join in the fun, both children and adults, as they proved by organising various events, including this sack race, at the fun Jubilee celebrations held at Grenville Green, Aylesbury.

Parties to celebrate the Queen's Silver Jubilee came in all forms but almost always there was special entertainment laid on to keep the children amused, as here in Chaucer Driver, Aylesbury.

A wave for the camera from those taking part in Jubilee celebrations at Hartwell.

What better place to hold a Jubilee celebration than outside a village pub? At least it gave the mums and dads the chance to have a refreshing drink as the youngsters had their own celebrations, just as they did outside the Bell Inn at Chearsley in June 1977.

Roads around the village of Brill were clogged one night in June 1977 as hundreds of people tried to make it to Muswell Hill for the lighting of a beacon to mark the Queen's Silver Jubilee, a celebration watched by this trio who were undeterred by the wind and rain, or the traffic queues.

Processions were all part of the Jubilee festivities, such as here at Long Crendon.

In the grounds of the Rothschild Arms at Aston Clinton this was the scene in June 1977 as villagers celebrated the Silver Jubilee.

Fancy dress was a popular way of celebrating the Silver Jubilee and a real effort was made by many, such as this group pictured at Westcott.

Go for it lad! A sports day was part and parcel of the Jubilee fun at Quainton.

The people of Haddenham, young and old alike, turned out in force to mark the Queen's Silver Jubilee with a carnival procession.

Themes to mark the Silver Jubilee were diverse, as this group showed at Longwick when their display recalled the Meadle Quakers who were well known in the local area for almost 100 years.

Crowds flocked to Princes Risborough to join in the Silver Jubilee celebrations which included a procession through the town centre.

Nothing, but nothing, could dampen the spirits of those attending Jubilee celebrations at Weedon, not even a sudden, heavy downpour.

This enthusiastic group of youngsters were among the hundreds who turned up at Green Park, Aston Clinton, in 1977 when Princess Anne opened a four-day exhibition to mark the Queen's Silver Jubilee.

Towns, villages and even individual streets, chose their own Jubilee Queens and Princesses as part of the Silver Jubilee celebrations in 1977 and some of those who featured in both *The Bucks Herald* and *The Bucks Advertiser* are remembered here, starting with two young ladies who caught the judges' eye at Weston Turville (*right*), the queen and her attendants, raising a glass to toast the occasion, at Waddesdon (*below*), the Jubilee Queen at Long Crendon (*next page, top, left*), the suitably crowned Queen of Hawthorn Close, Aylesbury, with her attendants (*next page, top right*) and the delightful group, and eventual winner, of the competition held at Haddenham (*next page, bottom*).

Princess Anne opened the Bucks Silver Jubilee Exhibition staged at Green Park, Aston Clinton, in June 1977 and was, we reported, delighted with everything she saw. The exhibition took the theme of 'Elizabethan Bucks 1952–77', and involved contributions from over 100 schools in the county as well as more than 100 voluntary organisations and groups. The exhibition, one of the most ambitious ever to be organised in Bucks, was attended by more than 2,000 schoolchildren over a period of four days.

Caught on camera was this youngster taking part in a torchlight event staged as part of the Bucks Silver Jubilee Exhibition held at Aston Clinton to celebrate the Queen's Silver Jubilee, just one of hundreds of Cubs from around the county who were involved in the exhibition.

It was to have been a flying visit when the Duke of Edinburgh arrived by a helicopter of the Queen's Flight at the Green Park Youth Training Centre at Aston Clinton one day in June 1974. But in fact he spent more than three hours meeting young people from all over Bucks who were involved in the various stages of the Duke of Edinburgh Awards Scheme. More than 1,000 spectators were there to welcome him and he spent time chatting to most of the 600 young people involved in the bronze, silver and gold sections of his Awards Scheme. He also took time out to chat to members of Aylesbury Red Cross who were on duty during his visit.

The famous royal smile of Queen Elizabeth the Queen Mother brought a ray of sunshine to the Kimble point-to-point races in March 1974 when crowds, who did not realise she would be attending, greeted her arrival with a storm of applause. As she walked to the paddock area she chatted to many of those attending the races which had been organised by the Pegasus Club and the King's Troop Royal Horse Artillery, and when the racing ended she presented the winners with their trophies.

The crowds crammed on to every vantage point to catch a glimpse of Princess Margaret when, in July 1970, she visited Aylesbury and spent some time touring the Friars Square shopping centre. 'There were thousands of shoppers and sightseers who had turned out to see her', we reported. After 'taking tea' with the Mayor and Mayoress, Alderman and Mrs H.D. Smith, and members of the Borough Council, the Princess went on to open a new £36,000 Church Army Youth Centre in Fairfax Crescent, Elmhurst, Aylesbury, where she met many of the young people involved in activities there.

Prince Charles piloted the helicopter which brought him to the opening of the International Stoke Mandeville Games for the Paralysed, held in 1977, the year of the Queen's Silver Jubilee. It was also the year in which the games celebrated its own silver anniversary. In his opening speech the Prince paid tribute to the work of the founder of the games, Sir Ludwig Guttmann, known simply as 'Poppa' (pictured right, below) and then went on 'walkabout', meeting not only many of the 600 disabled athletes from 35 countries taking part in the games, but also the crowd as well.

A new £1 million wing of Princess Mary's Hospital at RAF Halton was officially opened by another princess – Princess Alexandra – in November 1974. After unveiling a plaque the Princess spent more than four hours touring the hospital's corridors and wards, chatting to staff and patients.

Following on its success in winning the Queen's Award for Industry, the Molins Ltd factory at Saunderton received a royal visitor in November 1977, the Duke of Kent. The company produced cigarette-making machines which were exported around the world and during his visit, as well as meeting and chatting to staff, the Duke was able to see the machines in operation, producing 4,000 cigarettes a minute.

As patron of the Association of Spina Bifida and Hydrocephalus, the Duchess of Gloucester was at the Stoke Mandeville Sports Stadium in May 1976 to attend the 10th anniversary of the association. More than 1,000 parents and children from all over the country attended the celebrations and, after cutting an anniversary cake, the Duchess met many of them.

He could be forgiven a grimace. During a 1970s visit to RAF Halton, the Duke of Gloucester had the chance to see a range of RAF training facilities available there including the work of dental technicians. Ouch!

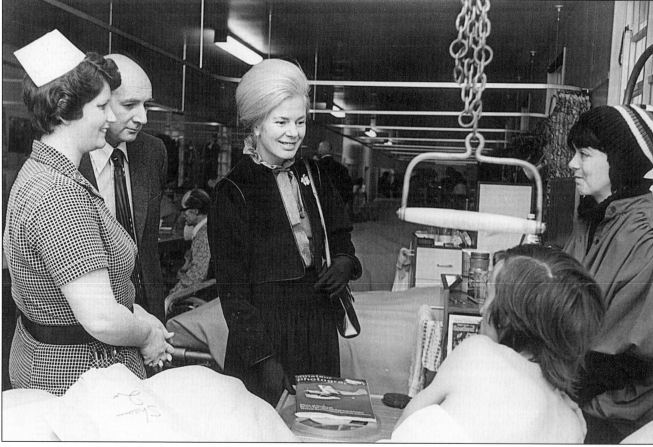

Her great interest in paraplegia, and the young disabled unit in particular, brought the Duchess of Kent to Stoke Mandeville Hospital in December 1977 when, as our pictures show, she spent all her time talking to patients, their families and staff. As one staff member was reported as saying: 'She was wonderful, she had time for everyone and her visit really cheered people up.'

Less than 12 months after visiting Stoke Mandeville Hospital, the Duchess of Kent returned, this time to the nearby Stoke Mandeville Stadium for a visit to the Aylesbury Red Cross Opportunity Playgroup. 'And her great affection for children was plain to see', we reported. She chatted to as many of the mums and the children as possible, including one who wanted to take his own picture of the Princess… so she borrowed a camera from one of our photographers and let him have a go! As she was leaving, she took time to look at a new playgroup vehicle and suddenly found a *Bucks Herald* photographer almost at her feet. He had slipped down an embankment while trying to take a photograph. As he scrambled to his feet the Princess told him: 'If you had hurt yourself, at least being here at Stoke Mandeville you would have been in the right place'.

CHANGING PLACES

This was one of the most historic buildings in Aylesbury town centre… until they pulled it down. The Bull's Head Hotel off Market Square (*right*) was the ideal setting for the arrival of a coach and horses in the 1960s, conjuring up images of how it must have been in its heyday when coaches stopped there frequently. But within less than a decade it was little more than a pile of rubble, having been torn down after it had been decided that the buildings as a whole were unsafe.

In September 1970 the last remnant of the hotel, the free standing metal sign at the front, was taken down (*below*). Estimated to weigh more than a ton it was broken up into pieces by Aylesbury Borough Council workmen. The site behind it was cleared (*next page*) and for a time was turned in to a car park. Then the United Reformed Church, seen to the left of the picture, was bought by compulsory purchase and, apart from the tower, was demolished to make way for the Hale Leys shopping centre which linked Market Square and High Street.

The Bull's Head is just one of the licensed premises which have disappeared over the years, many of which are recalled in the following poem:

The White Hart said to the Ram one day
Whilst having a chat with The Bear
'Who pulled the Bell at the Foresters Arms
and made the Green Man swear?'
'I think it was the Red Lion,' he said
As he gazed at the Rising Sun
The Saracen's Head and the Eagle knew
The Black Horse was the guilty one
The Horse and Jockey came trotting by
With the Plough and Harrow behind
The Windmill waved a Dark Lantern round
The New Inn and Grapes to find
The Falcon and the Greyhound
Clung to the Bricklayers Arms
The Nags Head wagged when Gullivers eyes
Admired Britannia's charms
Two Brewers and George went for a walk
But did not get very far
They called in at the Chandos
And then stopped at the Star

To watch Three Pigeons on the road
Strutting about the morn
Mixing with the Hen and Chickens
Picking up the Barley Corn
The Kings Head ached from wearing his crown
The Queen's was heavy as well
The Prince of Wales lunched at the Rockwood
And dined at the Bull's Head Hotel
The County and Borough thought they would like a trip
They did not want the Railway so they engaged a Ship
Coach and Horses from Derby Arms took them to
    Victoria dock
With Compasses and Cross Keys to open any locks
They also hired Millwrights and a few Oddfellows too
For they thought it very likely there would be repairs to
    do
The Plume of Feathers waved gently
The Buckingham Arms wound round
And the White Swan flew to join the crew
of the Hop Pole, New Zealand bound.

Hardly a busy High Street scene, but of interest here, on the left, is the former United Reformed Church, all of which was demolished to make way for the development of the Hale Leys shopping centre, apart from the impressive tower which, after renovation, was included in the new development. Opposite, and just visible, is the habadashers, Narbeths, which at the time was one of the oldest family businesses in the town. The shop premises, which extended through from the High Street to Cambridge Street, were destroyed by fire in the 1990s.

He may not seem to have a care in the world, perched as he is near the end of this crane, but not the same could be said for photographer Barry Keen who, in September 1972 scaled the dizzy heights – admitting afterwards that he had been 'terrified' – to take this bird's-eye view of High Street, Aylesbury. The crane was involved in the building of a new Co-op store, offices and underground car park.

From the top of a crane involved in building a new Co-op store in Aylesbury in 1972, this picture was taken of the lower part of the High Street clearly showing in the foreground the depot occupied by drinks company Dayla which, in 2001, celebrated its 150th anniversary. Formerly known as North & Randall, it is one of Aylesbury's only remaining owned and run family businesses. In the distance, near the centre, it just possible to pick out what was the site of the Aylesbury Technical College which has since been turned in to housing.

The 13th-century parish church of St Mary's in Aylesbury was closed in April 1978 and virtually gutted so that a major restoration project could start. It was planned, over the coming year, to spend more than £250,000 in changing it in to a dual-purpose building for both religious and social activities.

Changing places… quite literally. Planted to celebrate the birth of Prince Charles, this copper beech tree was given an instant transplant in February 1971 when it was moved from Hazell's Corner, as it was known, off Park Street, Aylesbury and found a new home in the cobbled Market Square. It had been planned to move it on to a new roundabout being created at the junction of High Street, Tring Road and Park Street, but this site was not ready.

With the silver trowel that he had used to lay the first brick of the first house on the Bedgrove Farm Estate in Aylesbury in September 1959, Mr Leslie Snell, chairman of builders H.C. Janes Ltd, laid the last brick on the last house to be built by the company at a topping-out ceremony, in July 1973 and to celebrate shared a glass of beer with staff. With a total of 1,723 homes on the 300-acre site, Bedgrove was, at the time, the largest housing estate of its kind in the country.

An Aylesbury pensioner is pictured here standing among the demolition debris of St John's Church which once stood in Cambridge Street. For Frederick Tofield there was more reason to mourn its passing than most, he was once a choirboy there and could recall the days when so many people attended that the front pews had to be booked in advance. The red brick church was pulled down to make way for redevelopment.

A sign of changing times came in Kingsbury, Aylesbury, early in the 1970s when bus shelters there were demolished. For many years Kingsbury had been used as a main bus collection point but, with the redevelopment of the Friars Square shopping centre and provision of a new, underground bus station, they became redundant.

At one time they were among the largest employers in Aylesbury and their chimney stacks a familiar sight on the skyline, as this atmospheric shot shows. But times change and International Alloys, which were once along the Bicester Road, relocated elsewhere. The factory and the stacks were demolished and the site is now an industrial estate and home to a variety of companies.

Taken in 1975 this aerial shot shows the new look centre of Aylesbury including the Friars Square shopping centre, multi-storey car park and Bucks County Council tower block on the right hand side while on the left is the Civic Centre, the cattle market and, beyond those, the Aylesbury canal basin.

Taken more than 20 years ago, this aerial picture shows how times change… and continue to do so. Running from the right-hand corner is the Tring Road and on either side, approaching the roundabout, are entrances leading in to factory premises occupied by printers and bookbinders Hazell Watson and Viney, at one time the largest private employer in the town. The factory has since closed, with the loss in total of more than 1,500 jobs, the Victorian buildings to the left of the picture, immediately opposite the roundabout, have been demolished and replaced with an industrial estate, while the bulk of the HWV buildings on the opposite side of the road have been pulled down and turned in to a supermarket site. Within the V-shape created by High Street and Park Street are the factory premises of Nestle which closes this year, 2002. Running across the centre of the picture is the Aylesbury Arm of the Grand Union Canal with Stocklake above.

Once known simply as the Bucks Lunatic Asylum – there was even a street in the village known as Asylum Road – here can clearly be seen the extent and scale of the former St John's Hospital at Stone as it was in the 1970s. With changes in care of those suffering mental health problems, most of the hospital buildings have disappeared to make way for housing development. One building to remain is the hospital chapel, visible right of centre...a lasting reminder of the use to which this vast site, with its 'rabbit warren' of buildings was once put.

This bird's-eye view of Aylesbury town centre was taken in 1975 – the Friars Square shopping centre had been completed (*left*), as too had the Civic Centre, indoor swimming pool and multi-storey car park (*right*). Centre of the picture, close to the roundabout, are the offices of *The Bucks Herald* and *Bucks Advertiser*, while the area in the foreground, once home to The Aylesbury Brewery Company and others, was set to change dramatically as well in the coming decades.

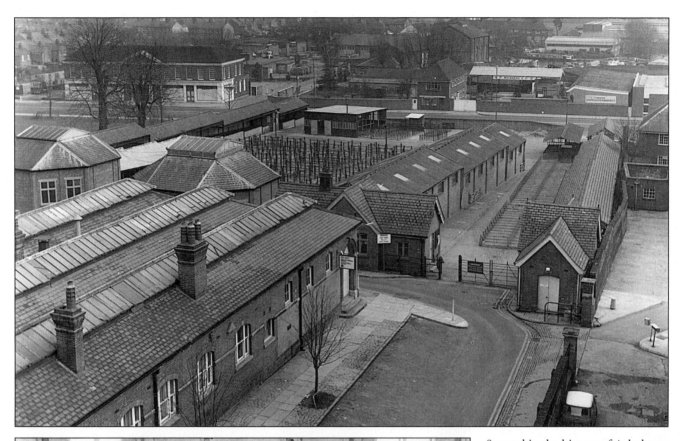

Steeped in the history of Aylesbury was the cattle market which, in our first picture (*above*), is shown as it was in 1970, looking towards Exchange Street, with, on the left the Aylesbury Borough Council offices. Beyond this building – now the site of the Civic Centre – are two buildings, known by many simply as 'the round houses' which is where the auctions took place each week (*top left*), while the final photograph in this trio (*bottom left*) shows the market, looking from the Exchange Street offices of *The Bucks Herald* in 1977, the year in which it was suggested that it might be better if a suitable site could be found for the market on the outskirts of the town, leaving this site available for redevelopment.

As well as the serious business side of the Aylesbury cattle market in Exchange Street, with auctions of sheep taking place around the pens (*top*), it was for some more of a family day out (*bottom*), as these 1970s pictures show.

In our first book, *Memory Lane Aylesbury: The Post War Years*, one of the pictures used was of the town centre area, including Market Square and Silver Street, before the bulldozers moved in and work began on creating the Friars Square shopping centre. This sequence of photographs shows what happened as the 1960s slipped away and a new decade was heralded-in with a development which was described on one occasion in *The Bucks Advertiser* as: 'The coming of Space Age Aylesbury to what was always the old-world centre of a small country town.'

The report on the biggest development in the history of the centre of the town continued: 'Modern, impressive buildings are rising up and gone are the centuries old streets that had to make way for progress.' Reduced to heaps of rubble were such well-known sights in the town as the Tinder Box, the popular Bourbon Street café, along too with the old offices of *The Bucks Advertiser*.

Continuing from the previous two pictures, 'More well-known names to disappear included two public houses, the Cross Keys and the Coach and Horses. The entire area covers former Bourbon Street, Silver Street, Brook Street, Great Western Street, Friarage Road, Friarage Terrace, Silver Lane and parts of Walton Street and Market Square.' The voice of protest was heard loudly and public inquiries were held, the new town centre being described as 'architectural fantasy' and 'ill-conceived and extravagant'. But nothing could stop what on the one hand was seen by many as being state-of-the-art development, but on the other as a planning travesty.

There was plenty still to be done when this picture was taken of the Friars Square shopping centre in 1967, but to bring life back in to this part of the town some of the shops were already open, with more yet to come, and the weekly open-air markets were being held in a special area created for them in the centre of the development. This meant moving the stallholders off the Market Square cobbles.

When critics talked about Aylesbury entering the space age with the Friars Square shopping centre development, they weren't far wrong, judging by this picture. The café building – later to become a Wimpey – caused a great deal of controversy and so too did the 'fountain', in the bottom right-hand corner of our picture, which, almost from the first moment it was used suffered from problems, including leaks, and was later removed.

This is one of a number of unusual photographs of Aylesbury town centre, taken from our own files, as it was in the run-up to the 1970s and while redevelopment work was in progress. They were taken by our own photographers who braved the heights of giant cranes being used in the building of the Bucks County Council tower block, and give a marvellous view of the surrounding area, much of which no longer exists.

This picture shows the scene as it was looking along Friarage Road. On the horizon can be seen the smoking chimneys of major employer International Alloys and immediately in front of them the row-upon-row of factory units occupied by agricultural machinery specialists New Holland. To the left is the area now occupied by the Safeway superstore, the Multi-Racial Centre, multi-storey car park and housing, while just off centre and at the bottom of the photograph can be seen the bell tower of what was the Railway Hotel. This was a building of unusual design which included gargoyles around the roof some of which were saved when it was demolished, and are now in the county museum in Aylesbury.

Compare this with the photograph *above* and notice that as work progressed the group of houses to the left of the Railway Hotel have disappeared and in their place the first signs of work going on to create the Friars Square shopping centre multi-storey car park. The tower building in the top left-hand corner is Aylesbury College.

Getting your bearings with this picture is quite easy – just look to the top for the unmistakable clock tower of the parish church of St Mary's. Clearly visible below this is Bourbon Street, but as for the remainder, all that has disappeared, swallowed up by the state-of-the-art town centre redevelopment.

Centre of this picture is the canal basin in Aylesbury but much of it would seem unfamiliar to most. In the top left-hand corner can be seen the chimney stack which was once a part of the Nestlé factory in High Street – a stack which was the last to be demolished in and around the town – while bottom left can just be seen the building which was the Aylesbury police station with the police garages on the opposite side of the road… an area of the town which, less than 40 years on, has changed dramatically.

The landmark in this picture of the town centre is, of course, the clock tower in Market Square and, not far from it, on the corner of Walton Street and the Square, the Bell Hotel. Less familiar are the triangular-shaped skylights on the roof of what were the premises of Lucas Furnishings and, in fact, all of the buildings immediately to the left of the square, including Silver Street, which were about to vanish as the bulldozers moved in.

What is that piece of green, open land right in the heart of Aylesbury? Well, many people still refer to a certain area of the town, just off Exchange Street, as 'the rec' – the old recreation ground. Immediately adjacent to the cattle market, a small open area of the site remains, for the moment at least, the remainder having disappeared beneath concrete as, in the 1970s, the centre of the town continued to be redeveloped.

The giant cranes in the background herald in a new-look decade for Aylesbury. The multi-storey Bucks County Council offices have been completed – a building nicknamed locally Pooley's Folly after the architect, Fred Pooley – but even amid the hustle-and-bustle of change there is time to reflect on more tranquil moments at the canal basin, part of the Aylesbury Arm of the Grand Union Canal, which, in the new millennium, looks set to become a major feature of the town centre.

As the 1970s approached, our newspapers had the foresight to record what areas of the town – which it was known would change – looked like at the time, such as these views over Southcourt, Aylesbury. The Aylesbury to Marylebone line is seen (*top*) with the branch line running towards Princes Risborough and particularly noticeable is the huge amount of open land to the left of the picture which has since become home to the offices and also the Aylesbury Magistrates Court. Our second picture shows a similar view looking over the railway station itself and showing the buildings which at the time were the old maintenance sheds for steam trains. The large area of open land in the foreground was to become the factory site for hair care specialists Schwarzkopf while, to the right of the picture, is the site of what is today the maintenance depot for the turbo trains used by Chiltern Railways.

PEOPLE AND PLACES

People were taking to the streets of Aylesbury in the 1970s to make their opinions known. It was, we reported, one of the quietest demos that the town was ever likely to see – 120 members of STEP – the 'Stop the Eleven Plus' campaign – who turned up one day in June 1971 (*top*) in the Market Square to protest as members of Bucks County Council went in to a meeting. They were demanding the introduction of comprehensive education throughout Bucks and handed-in a petition containing 8,263 signatures.

Six months later it was the turn of students from three colleges, including Aylesbury College of Further Education (*bottom left*), to voice their protests over government plans to reorganise student union grants. They also came from colleges at Chalfont St Giles and Slough. They are seen here marching along the High Street and note the films that were showing at the time at the Granada (which was later to become a bingo hall) – Anatomy of Love along with Wild, Willing and Sexy.

In June 1974 nearly 200 off-duty nurses from five local hospitals (*bottom right*) marched through Market Square protesting over pay and working conditions. Their march took them from the Royal Bucks Hospital to the Divisional Conservative HQ in Walton Street where they expected to meet local MP, Timothy Raison. But he wasn't there. Later Mr Raison said he had not been told the nurses were coming to see him. 'I had no idea I was expected to meet them, no one told me,' he said. Among their demands, the nurses wanted a starting salary of £2,000 a year for staff nurses and £3,000 for sisters and charge nurses.

The nurses' protest over pay in 1974 in Aylesbury may have been a serious one but there was still time for a smile as well… and our photographer was there to record the moment.

Threatened cuts in spending on education brought hundreds of teachers out to protest at a mass rally held in Market Square, Aylesbury, in February 1977, organised by NALGO, the National Association of Local Government Officers. One placard summed up the feelings and fears of many, which read simply: 'Cut the money, cut the standard'. But for some who turned up to support the teachers (*bottom*) there was time to take a break from listening to the union speakers and instead enjoy a nice cuppa.

An offshoot of a national postal strike meant that motorists had to call at the Aylesbury motor taxation office personally to renew the tax for their cars and long queues quickly built up outside the Walton Street premises as this scene one day in February 1971 shows. Many had travelled from around the county, including High Wycombe, Amersham and Slough, and were in for a long wait. Local postal workers set up their own strike HQ at the Aylesbury Labour Club in Castle Street and were demanding more pay.

Those in this line up were pictured outside the Cambridge Street fire service headquarters in Aylesbury in November 1977 on the first day of what was to turn into protracted and sometimes bitter strike action, taken nationally, over a 30 per cent pay claim. Forty-two members of the Fire Brigades Union were involved and their message was clear: 'If property is damaged or lives lost, it will not be the firemen to blame but Home Secretary Mr Merlyn Rees'.

Souper! To toast the 100th anniversary of the opening of the Nestlé factory in High Street, Aylesbury – which, when first established was known as the Anglo-Swiss Milk factory – what better way to do it than by sampling some of the products made there when the celebrations took place in 1970. Local dignatories and company bosses were obviously pleased with the taste of the soups they were trying.

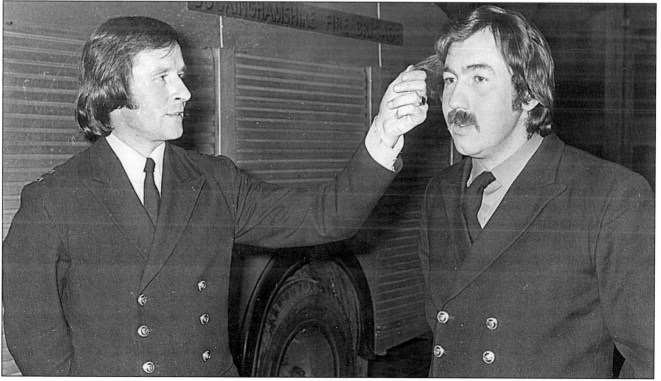

There was something of a hairy problem at the Aylesbury Fire Station in Cambridge Street in February 1970 – a number of the firemen, including Sub Officer Keith Algar and Fireman Bernard Hillyard (pictured here), had been told in no uncertain terms to get their hair cut or face disciplinary action. The firemen thought this was an intrusion into their private lives, the fire authority feared long hair could be a safety hazard.

Well known local character Esme Ward, who for 17 years had been housing unwanted and stray animals on land at her home in Bishopstone Road, Stone, was planning to move from the area and was preparing for what she had named 'Operation Noah's Ark' – moving all 130 animals, as well as her own belongings, to a 75-acre farm in Wales. In August 1970, as she made her plans, we reported the animals included not only cats and dogs but also ducks, doves and even a donkey. 'She will be greatly missed because of all the work she has done', it was reported.

Home for a family of six was this former tool shed, measuring just 18ft by 6ft and with no sanitation and just one electric light bulb, recorded a *Bucks Herald* front page story in March 1970. The husband and wife, with their children aged two years upwards, had been living with relatives but had been asked to leave. The only accommodation they could find was the tool shed, surrounded by rubbish, in London Road, Oving. They appealed to Aylesbury Rural District Council but, at the time the story appeared, the authority had been unable to find them somewhere suitable to live.

Wearing a blue velvet suit, a Royal College of Surgeons tie, his OBE and smoking a giant cigar, television personality Jimmy Savile, a regular visitor at Stoke Mandeville Hospital, was there on this day in October 1976 to present certificates, badges and awards at a nurses prizegiving. Although his mother – known to him as 'The Duchess' – had died only recently, Jimmy said he had been determined not to miss the awards ceremony.

It was a familiar site in and around the wards of Stoke Mandeville Hospital at Christmas, a visit by a choir made up of nurses to entertain the patients. And entertainment was certainly not lacking in the year this picture was taken, 1969, as just shortly before the hospital had been visited by a recording team for the BBC1 programme *Spoonful of Sugar* including Harry Secombe, Frankie Vaughan, Michael Aspel and Derek Nimmo.

It was thought to be the biggest charity walk that Aylesbury had ever seen – a trek from the town to Westcott and back to raise money for Help the Aged and the Aylesbury and Princes Risborough Division of the British Red Cross Society. Nearly 300 people paid 5p each in May 1971 to take part including MP for Aylesbury Timothy Raison and town Mayor, Alderman H.D. Smith, both of whom completed half the route. More than £1,600 was raised.

Spending 24 hours perched alone on top of a telegraph pole, some of it during torrential rain, would not be everyone's idea of how best to spend their spare time. But that's just what six people did in February 1972, doing it on a rota system of a day at a time each, to raise money for the McIntyre School for handicapped children at Wingrave.

'Aylesbury needs Jesus'. That was the message shouted across Market Square, Aylesbury one Saturday in February 1972 as a crowd of several hundred people took part in a 'Stand For The Light' act of Christian witness which was aimed mainly at young people. The only incident happened when, while gospel songs were being sung from a stage near the clock tower, a man had to be dragged away after he began shouting obscenities.

For the first time in six years the Whaddon Chase Hunt was able to follow its traditional 'meet' in Winslow Market Square on Boxing Day 1969 with a hunt and, it was reported, it proved to be a success with a 'kill' later in the day. Hundreds of spectators turned up to support the hunt and to see the hounds led into the square by the Master, Mr Dorian Williams.

This was the scene in September 1973 when, once again, the Bucks County Show – one of the largest one day shows of its kind in the country – was held at Hartwell on the outskirts of Aylesbury. For many years the show took place in the grounds of the historic Hartwell House, which can be clearly seen on the left and which, in more recent years has been turned in to a hotel, the show having moved to another site close to Weedon. But whereas the weather conditions on this day appear to have been fine, that was not always the case as our second picture, taken the following year, shows.

With thousands of visitors attending the show it was inevitable, as in this case, that if there had been rain before and during the show then there were likely to be problems and it was nothing unusual to see vehicles having to be towed from the site, through feet of mud, by tractors. It is obvious why this particular vehicle caught our photographer's eye, the number plate: Oh Jim.

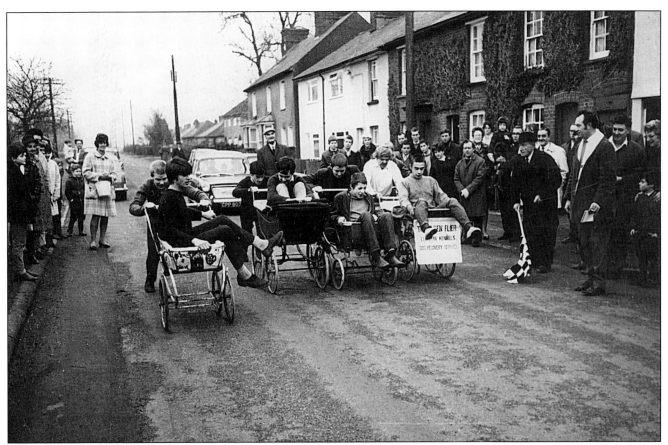

Organised by members of Aston Clinton Football Club, this was the annual pram race which took place on Boxing Day 1969 and which began from outside the Rothschild Arms in Weston Road. Those taking part who were old enough were expected to stop on the way at each of the village pubs and down half a pint. In all £12 was raised for club funds.

Aylesbury Round Table members had already spent the £500 needed to buy a baby incubator for the Royal Bucks Hospital in the town and were pinning their hopes on a donkey derby held at Weedon in September 1970 to recoup the money. And they weren't disappointed. More than 1,000 people supported the event and the money raised was £50 more than the cost of the equipment.

Here's a bird which must have taken the wrong turning. Aylesbury may be about 100 miles from the sea in any direction, but this puffin, a native of the north Atlantic, obviously didn't realise this. It was found on farmland outside Aylesbury in July 1977 and housed temporarily in a garage belonging to RSPCA inspector Charles Norris before being released nearer to home.

A house in Pemberton Close, Aylesbury may have been home to Les and Sue Stocker, but, as this picture of Les taken in June 1979 shows, it was also where a wide variety of animals and birds, which had been rescued locally, could be found as well. The couple set up the Aylesbury Wildlife Hospital here but were later to transfer to purpose built accommodation at Haddenham, the first wildlife hospital of its kind in Europe.

Each year, for as long as many people can remember, a carol service has been held in the Market Square, Aylesbury, over the Christmas period. And 1976 was no exception as this picture clearly shows, looking as it does towards the top of the square with the statue of Civil War hero John Hampden – in its original position – in the top right-hand corner.

While out driving along country roads through Kimble one April day in 1978, our photographer happened across this scene with the road blocked, not by cattle or sheep as one might expect, but rather by hounds from the local hunt out for some exercise.

This used to be quite a common scene in Aylesbury when the town could boast of having its own cattle market. It was nothing unusual for cattle and sheep to escape and for traffic to be held up, as with this incident in March 1977, when these animals decided that, rather being penned in the market, they would go for a quiet stroll along Exchange Street and Walton Street. To the right are the premises once occupied by the Cogger & Hawkins garage which is now the site of the Blue Leanie (a glass office building so called because it leans in different directions), which is home to the towns largest private employer, Halifax, Equitable, Clerical Medical.

Shoppers in the centre of Aylesbury just couldn't believe
their eyes when, one chilly November morning in 1976, a
baby elephant was brought in to the Market Square and
immediately began to get a little overfriendly with some of
the locals. And they were even more stunned when a blonde
in hot pants appeared among them and began to strip,
eventually posing topless with the elephant. It was all in the
name of publicity for a production of the play *A Thousand
Clowns* which was being staged at the Civic Centre later that
week. But the topless model did not stay that way for long. Police officers were quickly on the scene and wrapped her in one
of their own raincoats before taking her, and the organisers of the stunt – but not the elephant – to Aylesbury police station
where, after a warming cup of tea, they were all released without charge.

The organisers could not believe the success of the first Halton Show – held on the airfield of RAF Halton – in August 1971. Planned to raise money both for RAF and civilian charities they had no idea how many people would turn up to support what was essentially a motor show with more than 90 vehicles on display having been provided by local garages. In fact more than 5,000 attended and more than £1,500 was raised. Such was its success it was decided to make it an annual event and, while the motor show continued, the number of other attractions, including aerial displays, continued to grow as was seen in 1977 when among those taking part were the world famous Red Arrows whose display included a new manoeuvre called simply Jubilee to celebrate the Queen's Jubilee year. There was also a fly past by the Memorial Flight of a Lancaster, Spitfire and Hurricane and this year around 25,000 people attended and £7,500 was raised.

With a full head of steam, these railway enthusiasts were able to enjoy the sounds and smells of steam rail travel along a section of track at the Buckinghamshire Railway Centre, Quainton, during an open day in 1972.

Steam trains come in all sizes at the Quainton-based Buckinghamshire Railway Centre as visitors to an open day in April 1977 discovered.

Seventy years after it was built, and two years since the line was last used, the railway bridge at Woodham on the A41 Aylesbury to Bicester Road was finally demolished this day in January 1978 – work which caused traffic chaos with all vehicles using roads through nearby local villages instead. But for some the road closure brought a benefit. 'Children from the villages took the opportunity to use the empty road for skateboarding', it was reported.

We just could not resist using this picture when we came across it in our files. This was a scene at the Ex-Services Club in Walton Street, Aylesbury, one night in June 1974 when more than 200 people attended – and thoroughly enjoyed – the first old time music hall to be staged there. Among those appearing on-stage was the famous Irish tenor, Joseph Locke.

What a great turn out – and don't the smiles on their faces tell the story. This was a Darby and Joan Club tea party taking place in Haddenham in 1971.

If you had gone down to Doddenhall Woods near Grendon Underwood on a May weekend in 1973 you may well have been in for a surprise… camouflaged youngsters scurrying through the trees and bushes on mini-military exercises. They were Army Cadets from the 14th Waddesdon and Buckingham unit who were taking part in their first survival camp.

Out for a stroll, hand-in-hand, through the pretty village of Monks Risborough were these three youngsters who caught the eye of our photographer one summers day in the mid-1970s.

Always time for a chat. Well, at least there was in the 1970s as this delightful picture, taken in Church Lane, Weston Turville.

As the Royal British Legion standards were lowered at the Remembrance Day parade and service held in Market Square, Aylesbury, in November 1978, the first wreath was laid at the war memorial by chairman of Aylesbury Vale District Council, Councillor Mrs Edna Embleton. She was accompanied by her attendant and mace bearer, John Eagle, who wore his new uniform for the first time.

'These young Cubs joined their elders in paying tribute at Aylesbury war memorial to those who died to ensure they could grow up in a hate-free, fear-free society', said *The Bucks Herald* report of the Remembrance Day parade and service in November 1978.

No, No, No! That was the cry which went up in the Market Square, Aylesbury, one Saturday in October 1979 when yet another protest was called at plans to site a third London airport in leafy Bucks. The rally had been organised by members of the Aylesbury branch of the Wing Airport Resistance Association (WARA). A county-wide petition had been organised and more than 62,000 signatures had been collected.

The bench to the left of the picture, which had been reserved for the Old Contemptibles, may be empty but that is only because those who did attend the Remembrance Day parade and service in Market Square, Aylesbury, in 1976 were waiting their turn to lay a wreath at the war memorial. Pictured approaching the memorial is Freeman Harold Crookes, the wreath laying being watched by more than 500 people. The following week, as happened for many years, a Festival of Remembrance was held at the Civic Centre, organised by the county branch of the Royal British Legion. The Aylesbury Sea Cadets display team were among those taking part.

They were dancing in the streets… and why not? After years of protest, argument and debate, scenes like this were typical when it was announced that plans to build a third London airport in Bucks had been shelved.

For some prayer, and quite moments of reflection, were the way to mark victory in the battle over the siting of a London airport on their doorsteps, as these pictures taking in the village of Cublington show.

The message in both these pictures is clear I and illustrate that everything possible was done – even to enlisting the help of a baby elephant – to make plain the opposition there was in the area to any plan for a third London airport to be built locally. It was to be a long battle but, from beginning to end, those planning the scheme were told simply to 'Shove Off', as they were at Stewkley, while in Aylesbury High Street, just three words summed it up: 'No Airport Here'. And you don't want to upset an elephant, do you? After all, they never forget.

There was, thankfully, no more need for threatening banners such as these… and there were many of them. So much of the protest paraphernalia which had been such a part of the fight against the siting of a third London airport in Bucks, which would have affected many villages around Aylesbury, was consigned to the flames as giant bonfires of celebration were lit when it was announced the plans had been shelved.

He was quite a character. Having lived in Wingrave all his life, 90-year-old Ernest Rickard, a member of the villages Sunshine Club, was only too keen to get on his bike for a ride around to see family and friends as this picture, taken in March 1973, records. His recipe for a long life was simple: 'Hard work and a contented mind', he told our reporter.

FROM FIRE TO DROUGHT...
DISASTER STRIKES

A whole section of Southern Road, Aylesbury, was in danger of being destroyed by fire when thousands of pounds worth of damage was caused in March 1976 to a storeroom and office accommodation belonging to Elm Engineering Ltd. The roof of the building burned quickly and collapsed and eight water jets were used to bring the fire under control. Local firemen were praised for the way they had tackled the flames and prevented them from spreading.

Rushing to a fire in a mail coach at Cheddington station ended in disaster for the four-man crew on board this fire engine in April 1975. It skidded on the icy road and plunged in to a ditch at Lower Icknield Way, Aston Clinton. No one was injured and a second vehicle was quickly dispatched from Aylesbury to the railway station to bring the fire, which was among newspapers and letters on their way from Euston to Glasgow, under control.

A special watch had to be kept on this lorry which was involved in a collision with another vehicle outside the County Arms, Stone, in December 1975. Many of the beer bottles it was carrying were smashed but many remained undamaged, as did the barrels of beer. While the clearing up operation went on, which meant traffic had to be diverted, the police made sure that none went missing.

Regulars and villagers rallied round to tackle a blaze which almost completely destroyed the Swan, the only pub in Grendon Underwood in April 1977. Many returned after the fire at the thatched public house had been put out to lend a helping hand with the clearing up operation.

''Ello, 'ello, 'ello, what do we have here then?' The driver of this lorry obviously misjudged the size of this delightful looking creature, a white hart standing above the entrance to a pub of that name in Exchange Street, Aylesbury, and, having knocked the fittings off one side one day in 1971, had to wait there under the watchful eye of the law, until the well known pub emblem could be safely put back in to place.

A mother grabbed her year-old child and ran for safety as fire broke out in a council house at Grenville Road, Aylesbury, one day in April 1970. Her husband and three-year-old son also escaped as the house – one of the 'steel' houses built immediately after the war – went up in flames, the damage being so bad that nothing could be salvaged. The children were comforted by police officers as the fire was brought under control.

Hundreds of hedge, gorse and grass fires swept the Vale of Aylesbury during the drought conditions which came with the heat wave of the summer of 1976. Scenes such as these at Great Hampden were nothing unusual as fireman tackled flames in woodland, fields and even next to busy roads, with the public being urged not to drop anything, especially cigarettes or matches, which might ignite the tinder-dry ground.

More than 1,200 chickens died after fire swept through a modernised poultry unit at Ridgebarn Farm, Cuddington, in January 1974. These two chickens were the only survivors and, as well as the poultry the fire, believed to have been caused by an electrical fault, destroyed over £2,000 worth of equipment.

It was the worst fire seen in Aylesbury for many years. In January 1973 a total of 40 firemen – four of whom were slightly injured – spent several hours bringing under control a blaze which completely gutted the Aylesbury Discount Warehouse and which spread to the workshops of Benzole Motors Ltd.

It had been the coldest night on record for almost 30 years and for much of it this horse, Joey, was almost submerged in freezing mud at Lower Brook Farm, Worminghall. Firemen and farm hands joined forces to save the animal on an equally cold morning in January 1970.

Heave ho! Life for a fireman in a rural community does not always mean being called to fires or traffic accidents. Animal rescue plays a big part as well, a typical incident in the 1970s, caught on camera by our photographer, being this successful attempt to save a heifer at Grove Farm, Wendover, which had slipped into a muddy ditch.

Four cows were rescued from a slurry pit by two fire brigade crews in July 1979 at Model Farm, Upper Winchendon. It took several hours to bring the animals, each worth £350, to safety.

The Aylesbury to Oxford road was blocked for nearly four hours this day in July 1977, and traffic on other roads around the town came to a standstill, after a tractor and trailer carrying 250 bales of hay caught fire close to the entrance to Aylesbury College. It was thought the blaze started after a cigarette was carelessly thrown from a passing car.

A 77-year-old pensioner had a miraculous escape as she sat up in bed, waiting for her husband to bring her a cup of tea, in a room above the bar of the Crown Inn, Fort End, Haddenham, early one morning in July 1970. A double-deck car transporter, on its way to Aylesbury, crashed in to the corner of the 17th-century pub, shearing off a section of the building. The main bar had to be closed, but it was 'business as usual' later that day in the snug. Our second picture shows some of the damage caused to the bedroom.

The occupiers of this once pretty thatched cottage had to spend the night with neighbours after their home in High Street, Long Crendon, was virtually destroyed by fire in March 1971. While they tackled the blaze, firemen also managed to save furniture and other valuables from the building which were stored in a nearby church hall, 'as one of the occupiers was churchwarden there and had the keys to that building', it was reported.

Thar she blows! Workmen laying cables in Tring Road, Aylesbury, in November 1972 caused havoc when they damaged a water hydrant. Water shot 15ft into the air, drenching a wide area, and for a time the busy road was closed to traffic. In the top right-hand corner can be seen the premises of Adams Garage, Aylesbury, one of the longest established family businesses in the town.

The driver of this vehicle had a narrow escape when his articulated tanker loaded with domestic fuel oil jack-knifed and overturned on the Winslow-Buckingham road in April 1971 and burst into flames which shot 200ft into the air.

It was a miracle that no one was killed, read the headline. But nine people were injured and three cars written off after colliding near the Hanstead Stud on the road between Aylesbury and Whitchurch in June 1970. It was believed one vehicle had gone out of control, collided with another coming in the opposite direction which then somersaulted and struck the third car.

This was the scene which greeted fire crews in March 1971 when they were called to Dinton where an articulated lorry carrying a ton of wooden planks had collided head-on with a double decker bus. Of course they feared the worst. 'But everyone had a miraculous escape from death', read our report. 'It did take an hour-and-a-half to release one passenger who was trapped inside and one woman was thrown through the front top floor window on to the road. But there were no injuries more serious than a broken leg'.

All he did was to leave his car parked in Walton Street, Aylesbury, one December morning in 1972 and pop into a local newsagents for a paper. It was then that the car was struck and run over by a USAF articulated lorry which was on its way to Upper Heyford to deliver Christmas mail to American service personnel there. The car burst into flames and it was not long before crowds had gathered who were warned by police to keep at a safe distance. No one was seriously injured.

The driver of this car lay injured for several hours before he was discovered in a field alongside the Fleet Marston road in April 1972. The car had gone off the road and was hidden from view by a hedge and trees. A passing police officer spotted papers strewn about in the field and went to investigate.

A load of scrap aluminium was strewn over a wide area of Walton Street, Aylesbury, when an articulated lorry turned on to is side along the gyratory system in April 1972. No one was seriously injured but the busy town centre road was blocked for more than two hours. The lorry had been on its way to International Alloys in Bicester Road, Aylesbury.

A 60ft length of safety railings along Walton Street, Aylesbury, were smashed down when this 20-ton articulated lorry turned on its side in October 1972 and slide along the raised pavement area opposite the Horse and Jockey pub. 'It is a wonder that no one was injured', said our report.

A police inspector was taken to hospital, although not seriously injured, after his car crashed in to the wall of an empty cottage on the road between Aylesbury and Thame in March 1972, close to the Bottle and Glass pub at Gibraltar. The car, which was badly damaged, also struck an electricity pole and local people were without power for three hours while repair work was carried out.

It was an inferno. That is how one reporter summed up a fire which swept through the 18th-century Crown Court buildings and the meeting chamber of Bucks County Council in the centre of Aylesbury one Saturday morning in February 1970. It was the court where, in 1964, the Great Train Robbers received a total of 573 years imprisonment for their part in a mail train robbery at Cheddington.

Of the fire we reported that: 'A thick column of dark smoke was pouring out of the buildings as the fire appliances reached the Market Square.

'Crowds began to gather and the Square provided a perfect arena for the hundreds of spectators who arrived over the next few hours'. But people did not just stand and stare.

Like Chris East, who at the time was a sub-editor with *The Bucks Advertiser* and is now editor of that paper, they 'mucked in' and, while firemen overhead tackled the flames, helped police and council staff rescue deeds, documents and even furniture from the buildings. 'I was on my way to a friend's wedding at the registry office close to the court building and noticed the smoke and the fact it seemed to be getting worse all the time,' said Chris.

He was joined by staff photographers and colleagues from *The Bucks Herald* who all helped cover the story. 'It was one of the worst fires I had ever seen, and possibly one of the worst ever in the town centre,' he said. Fire crews from a wide area attended and it was believed from the outset that it had begun, and took hold, in the main courtroom (*top*) which was gutted.

There was a constant threat from falling roof timbers and one fireman was slightly injured, and taken to hospital when one of the heavy timbers fell on him (*bottom right*). At one time fire crews were pumping between 800 and 900 gallons of water a minute on to the blaze which took much of the day to bring under control and dampen down.

Later the same day an 18-year-old youth appeared before local magistrates charged with arson. Work began immediately on restoring the historic building and this was completed and the court and council chamber reopened, in just over a year.

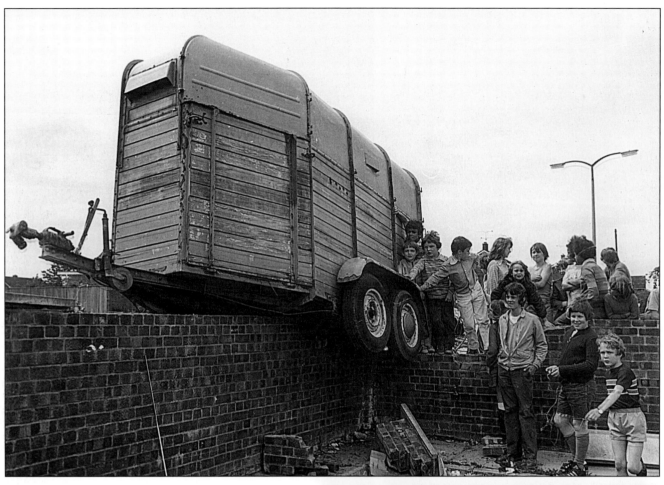

Children playing in Jansel Square, Bedgrove, Aylesbury, one day in June 1976 'got an unexpected thrill' but also had a lucky escape when an empty horse box, which was being towed by a Land Rover, came adrift and smashed into a wall bordering the square. Just a few minutes earlier the children had been playing close to the wall.

An Aylesbury woman had to be rescued from her car after it plunged 10ft into a brook near the Aylesbury Garage Centre in Walton Street in July 1976. The women, who was not badly injured, had driven onto the forecourt and then, said the police, she appeared to lose control of the vehicle.

CARNIVAL TIME

Damp but not downhearted. So what if it was raining, this was Aylesbury carnival day in July 1975 and, as always, the roads from Dunsham Lane, where the carnival procession began and the floats were judged, to the town centre were lined with people of all ages determined to enjoy the day.

1974 was another rather dismal year for Aylesbury carnival… but nothing could stop the crowds turning out in support. This picture is from the top of the Market Square and the floats are passing, on the left, what was the George public house. At the top of the picture, at the junction of Market Square with Kingsbury and Cambridge Street, there was a vacant area which separated two small pubs, the Harrow and the Barleycorn. Later these were to be joined together, and revamped, to create, what else, but the Harrow and Barleycorn.

Scenes from the carnival procession through the streets of Aylesbury in 1977 which was an occasion, being the Queen's Silver Jubilee, when a very special effort was made. The carnival was one of the highlights of activities in the town and for many years was organised by the towns Junior Chamber of Commerce. But when members of the chamber decided they could no longer continue, no one came forward to take on the months of planning and preparation and 'carnival day' came to an end. Among the floats on this occasion was one from Rediffusion who at one time were based in the town.

'As always the crowds turned out in force', it was reported of the 1970 carnival day in Aylesbury and there was plenty to see including 300 children taking part in the fancy dress section and more than 100 floats organised by local businesses, groups and organisations. Earlier there had been a carnival ball held at Hazells Hall and following the procession the popular 'Hobble on the Cobbles' was staged in the Market Square when local groups entertained hundreds of 'music lovers'.

These are just some of the 20,000 people it is estimated were in Aylesbury town centre in July 1971 to enjoy the town carnival. More than 1,000 people manned more than 90 floats in the parade which was led by the RAF Halton apprentices pipe band, and pubs around the town centre were doing a roaring trade – nearly 30 had been open since earlier in the day and there had been little if any trouble, it was reported.

These two little girls (*above*) were obviously enjoying themselves on one of the many floats at the Aylesbury carnival in 1975, while the tiny tot (*right*) seemed determined to take some snapshots of her own, having taken part in the fancy dress parade, while at the Edinburgh Playing Fields in Aylesbury where those who had watched and taken part in the procession had the chance to keep the carnival spirit going with various fun events, games and sideshows.

Three more scenes from the 1971 Aylesbury carnival – scenes which were typical each year with the crowds cheering and applauding each float as it made its way through the towns streets, recognising the effort and imagination which had been put in, often over many months, to make every float individual, and, of course, to catch the judges eye. *Top* shows nursing and medical staff from local hospitals – Stoke Mandeville, Manor House, Royal Bucks and Tindal – both on and off duty, *centre* was the entry from the Aylesbury Air Training Corp, while staff at Schwarzkopf in Aylesbury *bottom* took the opportunity, as so many did, to advertise their own products.

From a window at the Bell Hotel in Market Square, our photographer took these pictures of entries at the 1971 Aylesbury carnival which came in all shapes and sizes – from the large and rather crowded lorry being used by one local group who took a music hall theme, and won for themselves a first prize.

The rather less
inspiring entry from
the Aylesbury
Liberals.

CHILDREN OF THE 70S

Aylesbury Ex-Services Club in Walton Street held its first children's party in February 1971 when 140 youngsters, aged four to 10 thoroughly enjoyed their food and especially the entertainment, judging from our picture. As they left for home they were given gifts of fruit and sweets.

As part of a special 'Back to School' feature in *The Bucks Herald* in an edition of August 1972, these scenes were caught on camera at Bedgrove School, Aylesbury.

Will he… won't he? The pictures speak for themselves as these two youngsters, known only to us as Steven and Jane (*pictures above*), were caught on camera by our photographer Barry Keen in their own tunnel of love at the Quarrendon adventure playground in Aylesbury in 1974.

A special report with pictures looked at adventure playground facilities for youngsters in the area (*pictures right and left*) and stressed that they showed there was more to life than vandalism, football hooliganism and petty thieving.

It is the sort of photograph opportunity that no local Press photographer can resist. This charming young lady was caught on camera at the annual Weston Turville horticultural show held in August 1970.

Get a move on! A lettuce leaf feast was first prize in this snail race run at a garden party held at Trinity Church, RAF Halton in May 1971 to raise money for Christian Aid. The winner completed the four-foot table top course in a mere 14 minutes 25 seconds and its owner, seven-year-old Philippa Corderoy, (inset), who had owned and trained the previous years winner, was presented with a box of sweets.

They are having a great time. This was the scene our photographer found when he was invited along to take pictures of a party organised by the Abbey Playgroup, Aylesbury, in December 1973.

Four-year-old Kathie Young was in for a surprise when she turned up for school one day in October 1971. The delighted pupil was presented with a special certificate to celebrate the fact she was the 1,000th pupil to be enrolled at Chearsley County Primary School since it opened in 1880.

Whatever they're watching, it must be great fun. Staff of printers and binders Hunt Barnard in Aylesbury brought their children along one day in December 1979 for a Christmas party organised by the company.

This (*picture top right*) was a typical scene captured on film by our photographers during the heatwave and drought of 1976 – a welcome dip being taken in The Vale open air swimming pool in Aylesbury. And the young chap (*top right*) carrying, not just a fishing net but also a large fan to help him keep cool, shows just how hot it must have been as they made their way through Wendover during the scorching summer of that year. And note the fashions! But there was some respite (*bottom left*) and not even the organisers of the Weston Turville Church fete complained when it actually rained during their fund raising event in June of that year – rain which was obviously enjoyed by these two young stallholders Matthew and Amanda Wren.

It is all new to them but they still managed to raise a smile – their first day at Bedgrove School, Aylesbury, in September 1978.

Pupils of Broughton Junior and Infants Schools in Aylesbury turned out in force on 2 April 1970 to say 'cheerio' to their lollipop man Harry Woodward of Milton Road who had manned his position along the Tring Road for more than 16 years. Harry, a former printer, took on the job, which he said he loved so much, after retiring as a printer. To help him enjoy his retirement the staff, parents and pupils presented him with an armchair.

Putting their best feet forward these youngsters set off from the Congregational Church in Wendover one rather damp April day in 1970 to trek to Weston Turville, through Halton Village, and back again, to raise money for Christian Aid Week. Their sponsored effort raised a total of £100.

Our photographer just couldn't resist taking this picture of a group of 'fashionable' youngsters seen walking along Oxford Road, Aylesbury, on a sunny day in 1971.

For these three excited youngsters (*left*) there was the chance to have a sneak preview of the robes and regalia which would be worn by their grandma, as the incoming Mayor of Aylesbury, Alderman Mrs Zena Williams, prepared for the mayor-making ceremony in May 1971. There was a chance for youngsters from Southcourt First School to try on similar robes for themselves (*right*) even if they were far too large, when they visited the Mayors Parlour in Aylesbury town centre in October 1978 to learn about the history of the town.

Rather an unusual pose, but these youngsters from Haddenham C of E First School don't seem too bothered about being asked to hold up high a 6ft-long teak seat which had been presented to the school in July 1977 by the Parent Teacher Association to celebrate the Queen's Silver Jubilee. Money was raised through jumble sales and bazaars and it was felt it was better to present something that would be a permanent reminder of the celebrations rather than individual jubilee gifts for the children.

On this day in July 1972, the doors finally closed at what had been a landmark in the village of Nether Winchendon for nearly 100 years. The village school (*bottom*) was first opened in 1875 but, with falling roll numbers, it was decided it should be shut and the last 12 pupils (*top*) moved to other schools in the surrounding area. At an open day held just before the closure it was stressed that over the years the school and maintained the highest Christian standards.

This photograph of local youngsters was taken a long time before a certain politician coined the phrase, when referring to the unemployed of 'on yer bike' and it is obvious that the time they spent in 1970 passing their cycling proficiency test, with help from the local police, had been well worth while.

This was obviously one of those hazy, lazy days of summer and these youngsters had decided to make the most of it by enjoying a leisurely ride around the pretty village of Monks Risborough by donkey and trailer, one of the fund raising attractions at a fete held there in September 1978.

What a whopper… and nearly a record breaker too! Jayne Cleaver of Chearsley was in for a surprise on her eighth birthday in March 1976, when one of the chickens on the farm where she lived laid this giant egg weighing nearly half-a-pound, just short of the world record according to *The Guinness Book of Records*. One of our photographers left the farm rather embarrassed, the egg had broken. But to this day he refuses to say just what happened.

What a smashing group picture, taken by our photographer at Brownie Revels held in Aylesbury in July 1971.

Not difficult to guess what these youngsters, and their parents, are enjoying. Punch and Judy, of course. This was the scene at Hazell's fete in August 1979, one of the largest events of its kind in the area which was organised for staff of printers and bookbinders Hazell Watson and Viney, and their families. Most of the site has since been sold for housing.

There was plenty to choose from when this Guides fund raising bazaar was held in Aylesbury in November 1971.

Tally ho! Little Tracey Jones has a wave – and a smile – for the camera as she celebrates the fact that with her curiously named pony, Reeves My Measles, she had become the youngest rosette winner at the Tring and District Horse Association gymkhana held at Pendley in April 1974.

More than 3,000 people turned up for the first event of its kind in Aylesbury, a rock festival held at Rabans Lane which has since become an industrial estate on the outskirts of the town. Aptly named Rabans Rock, it was held in June 1973 and among those appearing on stage were local musicians Wild Willy Barrett and John Otway. It had been organised by Dave Stopps (*top, with headband*), founder of the Friars Club in Aylesbury, who went on to manage pop-star Howard Jones. Friars was recognised as being one of the best rock clubs in the country. The first club event was staged at Friarage Hall in Walton Street in June 1969 when just 150 turned up. Within four years it could boast a membership of 8,000. Also pictured on previous page.

He might well be shrugging his shoulders. After all, what was an 18ft tall wooden waterwheel doing next to Haddenham village pond as it was on this day in November 1974? John Cleese, who had just left the *Monty Python* team and was co-writing a new TV series, *Fawlty Towers*, had time to chat to villagers during the shooting of scenes for a Skol lager advert.

Six years later it was the turn of TV stars The Muppets – Kermit the Frog, Fozzie Bear and The Great Gonzo – to make use of the picturesque pond, in what was described by the film makers as 'a typical English village' for a film provisionally entitled *The Second Muppet Movie*. Among the 180-strong film crew was The Muppets creator Jim Henson, and 'a typically English gentleman actor' Robert Morley who had a cameo role.

Schoolchildren were given time off lessons to watch the filming and the only person who was disappointed, we reported, was one elderly gentleman who was heard to complain that his favourite Muppet, Miss Piggy, was not among the stars on the day.

Messages came in dozens of different ways… wrapped around a cigar, scribbled on a plate, a shirt and even a pair of panties. The Radio One Club arrived in Aylesbury one lunch time in January 1971 and more than 700 young people turned up at Hazells Club to take part in the 'live' two hour broadcast hosted by disc jockey Ed 'Stewpot' Stewart who was helped on occasions by local DJ and pop writer for *The Bucks Herald*, Dave James. A live performance was given on stage by The Troggs.

Journalist and TV personality Michael Parkinson joined an *Any Questions?* panel for a programme recorded at Stoke Mandeville Hospital in December 1974 which the BBC were planning to send out on their world service later in the month. But the man who was famous, as our front page headline pointed out, for his grin found time to visit many of the hospital wards and chat to patients.

Steam train driver John Carter and his fireman, Colin Copcutt, both from Aylesbury, found themselves among the stars of the BBC children's programme *Playschool* when an outside broadcast unit – along with programme hosts Johnny Ball and Sarah Long – arrived at the Quainton Road railway station to record a whole 25-minute programme in January 1976.

Returning by popular demand, the BBC TV comedy series simply called *Sykes* brought Eric Sykes, Hattie Jacques and Derek Guyler – who had just finished starring in the series *Please Sir* – to spend two days recording in the village of Aldbury in March 1972 for an episode called 'Sykes on a walk'.

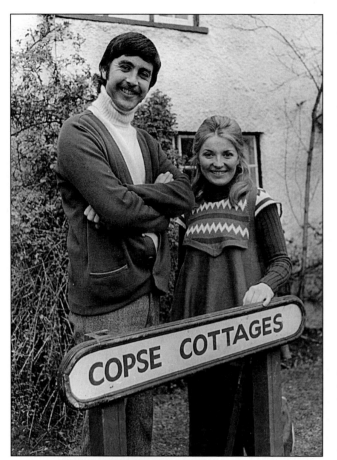

If you went looking for Copse Cottages at The Lee near Wendover in 1972, you would have been out of luck. The sign had been put up by the props department of the BBC while recording went on for four days to shoot outside scenes for a new television comedy *My Wife Next Door* starring John Alderton and Hannah Gordon. And if you happened to post a letter in a post box close to the sign, delivery would have been delayed. That was just a prop as well.

No prizes for guessing what entertainer Arthur Askey said to these members of the Granada Bingo and Social Club in Aylesbury when he met them during a visit in November 1973 – it had to be his famous catchphrase 'Hello Playmates'. He was 'the first big star' – in name if not in stature – to entertain club members and the 400 present enjoyed his performance so much they kept him on stage for over an hour, much longer than planned.

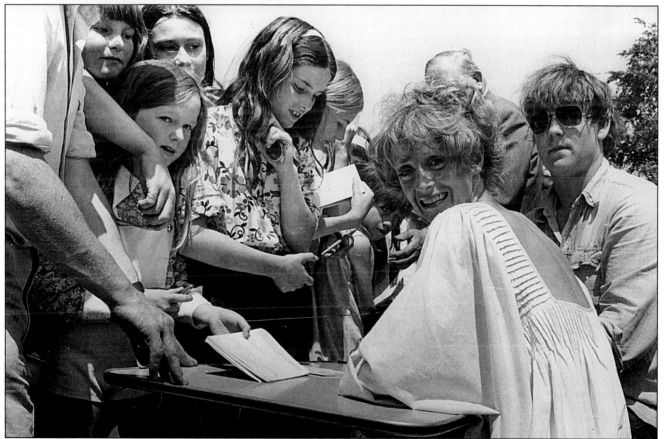

TV star Polly James, who at the time was playing Beryl in the popular BBC comedy series *The Liver Birds*, signed autographs at 2p a time after opening the Wendover carnival fete in June 1973, the money raised going towards a fund to build a swimming pool in the village. Held in the grounds of Wendover House School the fete attracted a record crowd of nearly 9,000.

Penny Lane, the 'singing star' of the TV series *Lunchtime with Wogan* said she was flattered to have been asked to become the official pin-up of Kestral Flight at RAF Halton. In May 1973, she visited the RAF station to meet the aircraft apprentices and tour the workshops

There was delight, tinged with disappointment, on the faces of many of those who turned up at Rabans Lane, Aylesbury, one Saturday afternoon in July 1975 for a concert organised by Aylesbury Junior Chamber of Commerce as part of the town carnival. Miming to their records were The Wombles – at least three of them – but they only performed for a short time which meant many arrived too late to see them. 'They were each paid £150 so we could only afford three of them. We booked three and three turned up,' said a Chamber spokesman.

They came Wombling down Aylesbury way in July 1975 and got up to antics on stage at a concert held as part of the town's annual carnival.

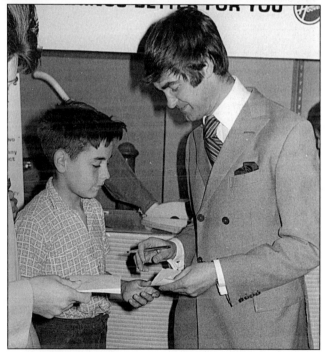

Our photographer had to go 'undercover', posing as part of the film crew, to hastily snap this picture early in 1971 of preparations being made to shoot scenes for what turned out to be the highly controversial Stanley Kubrick film *Clockwork Orange*. Kubrick banned all photographers from the Friars Square shopping centre which was chosen because it was state-of-the-art, one of the most modern centres of its kind in the country.

'Golly Gosh', his catchphrase, might well have been the first reaction of TV personality Derek Nimmo when he arrived to support a free show, organised by Eastern Electricity, and held at the Odeon Cinema in Cambridge Street, Aylesbury, in May 1970. Despite the fact that thousands of invitations had been sent out only 250 people attended to see cookery demonstrations and to meet the celebrity who, although there was a poor turn out, was kept busy signing autographs.

Fun-making turned in to film making when Terry Scott, June Whitfield and Peter Butterworth, complete with a BBC2 film crew, turned up at the annual Ashendon WI fete, held on the Playing Fields, in July 1971, to record an episode of Terry Scott's new series *Scott on Entertainment*. The assistant producer of the series lived in the village and suggested the fete would make an ideal setting for one of the programmes.

These local youngsters were among those who took part in a special Christmas edition of the much loved children's programme *Playaway* in 1973. They were set certain tasks to do in a temporary studio which had been set up in the Borough Assembly Hall in Aylesbury, while an 'outside recording unit' filmed scenes around the town including members of the Aylesbury Girls Brigade singing carols in the Friars Square shopping centre.

His bone mans rags were left at the studio as Harry H. Corbett – Albert in the TV series *Steptoe and Son* – donned a dapper shirt, trousers and cravat when he opened the Tring Junior Mixed Schools Swimming Pool Committee summer fete in June 1970. Over 4,000 people supported the event and a grand total of £1,117 was raised.

Puffing Maigret-like on his pipe, actor Rupert Davies, who lived at Penn in Bucks, took time out from recording an episode of *Fraud Squad* at the Elstree studios, to open the first Wendover fete to be held in the village for 38 years. The organisers were delighted that more than 4,000 people turned up to support the event and £750 was raised.

The France of Guy de Maupassant came to Waddesdon Manor, via the BBC, in November 1970. The grounds of the stately home were used as a setting for de Maupassant's *Bel Ami*, a classic serial which was to be screened on BBC2 the following year. Peter Sallis is pictured with fellow actor Robin Ellis.

Members of the North London branch of the Caravan Club, who happened to have set up in nearby fields during the April Bank Holiday in 1970, joined in Easter celebrations outside the Shoulder of Mutton at Owlswick which included the judging of a bonnet parade carried out by television personality Stubby Kaye.

Keeness, cheerfulness and effort – these were the things that impressed Brian Moore, football commentator with London Weekend TV, when he opened a sports rally for physically handicapped children at Stoke Mandeville Sports Stadium in July 1975. 'It would do a lot of professional sportsmen a lot of good to see the young people here today,' he said.

Formed early in 1970, the Wing branch of the Muscular Dystrophy Group of Great Britain held a major fund raising fete at Wing in August of that year (*left*) which was supported by comedian Roy Castle whose home was at Gerrards Cross. Accompanied by his three children, Daniel, Julia and Antonia, he opened the fete and spent more than two hours visiting the stalls and sideshows and, of course, signing autographs. The following year, in March 1971 (*right*) and playing the mellophonium, he was at a Princes Risborough garden centre, this time with wife Fiona, whose parents lived at Speen, to launch a scheme introduced by the Horticultural Trades Association to give help to amateur gardeners.

Not content with just helping to start a 10 mile sponsored walk in aid of the Bucks branch of the British Red Cross, disc jockey Jimmy Savile put his best foot forward and joined in as well. It was April 1974 and the walk began from the Stoke Mandeville Sports Stadium with Jimmy being given support by Councillor Mrs Freda Roberts, who, just the week before, had been installed as the first Town Mayor of Aylesbury following local government reorganisation. Entertainment both at the start and finish was provided by local group, The Paratones, consisting of past and present patients of Stoke Mandeville Hospital.

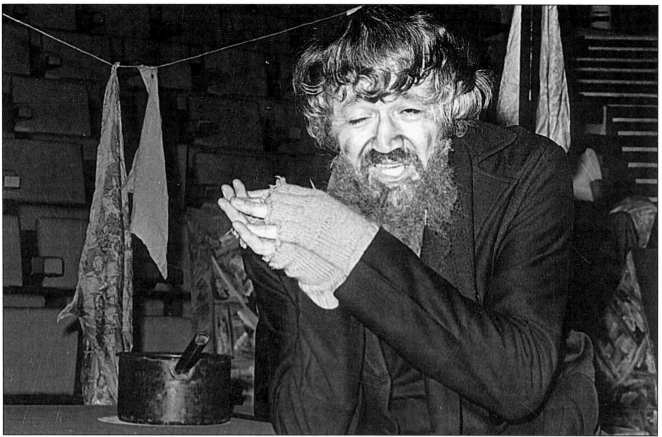

It was their 21st production and the first at the recently opened Civic Centre in Aylesbury which had replaced the Borough Assembly Hall. For their celebration production of the musical *Oliver*, members of ADOS – the Aylesbury Dramatic and Operatic Society – decided to perform it in the round. One of the 'stars of the show' was society stalwart Gordon Bishop who took on the demanding role of Fagin.

They were walking through Market Square, Aylesbury, with a pumpkin and look what it turned into! Well, that was the excuse of the Ugly Sisters – Philip Thurley and Gordon Bishop – when confronted by traffic warden Hilda Reeves. In fact the pair were publicising a production of *Cinderella* by the Aylesbury Dramatic and Operatic Society in 1972. In the background is part of the Friars Square shopping centre which has since been redeveloped.

Valerie Singleton, the *Nationwide* TV presenter, was the special guest at the Hartwell Riding School's gymkhana held in August 1976, to raise money for the Riding for the Disabled Club and is seen here presenting a rosette to Sarah Godliman.

Raising money for the British Heart Foundation and the Friends of Luton Town FC, the organisers of the annual Burston Charity Cross Country Event, held at Weedon asked comedian Eric Morcambe – 'the one with the glasses' – for his support and he was, he said, delighted to help out on 16 September 1976.

War hero Group Captain Sir Douglas Bader arrived in Aylesbury on 14 October 1976 to perform 'a very special duty' – the opening of a £35,000 adventure playground at Stocklake named after Jonathan Page, a voluntary worker at the nearby Manor House Hospital for the mentally handicapped. Jonathan had died at the age of 20 in a tragic canoeing accident.

The Batchelors – Con and Dez Clusky and John Stokes – were mobbed by hundreds of their fans when they visited Woolworths in the Friars Square shopping centre, Aylesbury, on 24 February 1977 to promote their latest single *Torn Between Two Lovers*. The trio's first hit had been 10 years earlier with *Charmaine* which sold over 250,000 copies.

Mum of four Ann Swaithe of Stratton Green, Aylesbury, was always likely to remember 1976 – it was the year that she was named as a finalist in the national Pub Entertainer of the Year competition. For some time Ann, whose act included impersonations of Elvis Presley, Bernie Winters and Frank Spencer, had appeared on stage with local group Rainbow but then she decided that comedy was her forte. And how right she was!

All eyes were on one person at a book fair held at Monks Risborough C of E Combined School in April 1979 – author Roald Dahl (*left*) who visited the school from his home at Great Missenden to officially open the fair and, of course, sign autographs.

The impressive whiskers give it away. Doffing his top hat in the style of a true gentleman is well known TV and film personality Jimmy Edwards who was caught on camera riding with a local hunt in January 1972.

Singer and entertainer Val Doonican – along with his famous rocking chair – was appearing at the Civic Centre, Aylesbury, in March 1978 and took time out to meet some of the 2,000 fans who watched two performances of his show which also starred Stan Boardman of the TV children's programme *Run Around*.

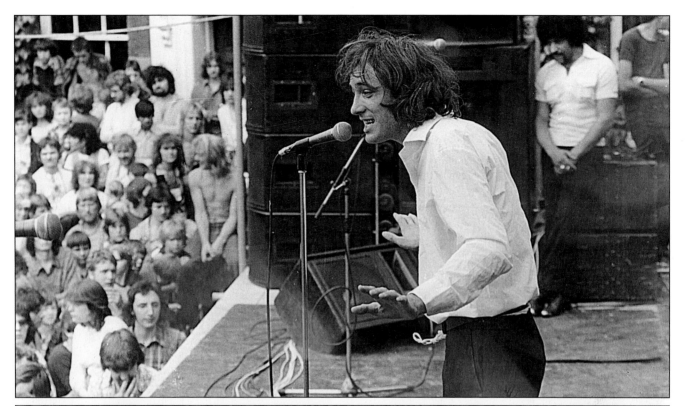

It was headlined on the front page of *The Bucks Herald* on 13 August 1978 as: 'Something the town can be proud of… and not a hint of trouble'. It marked the day that more than 12,000 people crowded into the town centre to see a free open-air pop concert by local musician John Otway whose record *Cor Baby, I'm Really Free* had made it into the charts. For local lad John it had been a rags to riches story with him having worked for a time in the town as a dustman but, just before the concert took place, buying for himself a silver and black Bentley. But, although he may have made a name for himself, he still bought many of his clothes from the local Oxfam shop, as he had always done.

For six years he had always given a free concert in the town but, following on the success of his record, he wanted to do something special as a way of saying thank you to all those who had supported him locally, and with the help of Friars Club organiser Dave Stopps, the one-off concert was arranged. The preparations, and the concert itself which included John up to his usual on-stage antics such as swinging on the scaffolding, was recorded for an ATV television programme to be broadcast later in the year.

Autograph hunters, mainly young girls, turned out in force when Miss England 1971 visited Woolworths in the Friars Square shopping centre, Aylesbury.

Adoring fans almost clambered on to the stage of the Civic Centre, Aylesbury, to guarantee they got his autograph, when radio and television personality Noel Edmonds, who at one time lived at Weston Turville, appeared there in September 1975.

There was an attentive audience when author H.E. Todd visited Elmhurst School, Aylesbury, in February 1978 to read to pupils some of his own works including *Changing of the Guard* which had been illustrated by a regular visitor to the Aylesbury area, fellow-author Val Biro.

POLITICIANS... AND YOU

Last minute Christmas shopping brought Prime Minister Edward Heath, who was staying at nearby Chequers, into Aylesbury town centre in 1973 – accompanied by a bodyguard of course. For a while he walked round the streets virtually unnoticed. 'But then a small group spotted him as he was joined by local MP Timothy Raison and he spent much of his time chatting and signing autographs', we reported. He visited a number of shops including Weatherhead's bookshop in Kingsbury and Woolworths in the Friars Square shopping centre (*bottom*). He took a break from shopping, and the crowds, to enjoy two halves of bitter at The Kings Head off Market Square.

Constant heckling – with razor sharp repartee from the deputy leader of the Labour Party, George Brown – provided a lively opening to the 1970 election campaign in Friars Square, Aylesbury, in June of that year. The lunchtime open air meeting had been called by the Aylesbury Labour Party in support of their candidate, Jim Mitchell, and the speeches were greeted by both cheers and boos, the latter often being much more audible.

Scuffles broke out in the Market Square, Aylesbury, in the early hours of a June morning in 1970 as the results of the General Election were announced from the steps of County Hall. On hearing that Conservative Timothy Raison (*bottom picture*) had scored a resounding victory over the opposition, with a majority of nearly 11,000, Labour supporters lashed out at some in the large crowd waving Tory banners. This man (*right*) – firmly in the arms of the law – was arrested and taken to Aylesbury Police Station but was not charged.

It may seem rather cramped, but this is where Aylesbury Borough Council once met, at the Town Hall, which was off the Market Square. Our picture (*top*) of the council chamber was taken in 1971 when the Mayor was Councillor Mrs Zena Williams. Next door to the town hall were the council offices (*bottom*) which, like the authority itself, were about to disappear. Both the Borough Council and the neighbouring Aylesbury Rural District Councils vanished in 1974, being merged into Aylesbury Vale District Council.

The offices themselves were to be demolished and the site used for the new Civic Centre buildings which opened in 1975. At the bottom of this short stretch of road, and clearly visible, are buildings which once formed a part of the town's cattle market. These too have long since gone.

It must have seemed to some that whenever Harold Wilson visited the Aylesbury area it rained! As leader of the opposition and accompanied by his wife Mary, he turned up in Berryfield Road, Quarrendon, Aylesbury, one day in July 1971, to open a fete organised by the local branch of the Silver Leaf Club – a fete which had to be moved indoors because of a torrential downpour. At the end of the day 'a grand total' of £76 had been raised.

Three years later, in September 1974, it was umbrella time again as Mr Wilson, now Prime Minister, arrived at the Stoke Mandeville Sports Stadium to open the first ever world games for the multi-disabled. On the right of the picture is Sir Ludwig Guttmann, founder of the games and president of the International Sports Organisation for the Disabled.

It was headlined: 'A word from the musical PM'. Who else could it be but Prime Minister Edward Heath who, one day in March 1971, toured the Aylesbury School of Music at the Aylesbury College of Further Education. With over 300 students and more than 40 junior school scholars, he told them: 'I was going to be a professional musician but I went wrong and went in to politics instead'.

Leader of the Opposition, Margaret Thatcher, received 'a spontaneous, friendly and somewhat crushing welcome' when she attempted a walk-about in Aylesbury town centre this day in December 1977. The scenes, it was reported, were a reflection of her popularity. Having earlier visited Stoke Mandeville Hospital she slowly made her way around the Market Square before arriving at the Civic Centre to address a conference of 300 supporters.

'Now look 'ere'. This was the scene in Market Square, Aylesbury on 26 April 1979 when Chancellor of the Exchequer, Denis Healey, faced a barrage of questions from the audience which had gathered by the steps of the clock tower to hear his speech in support of the Labour candidate for Aylesbury, John Power, in the run up to a general election. Before he left the town he was presented with a book about old Aylesbury by members of the Aylesbury Labour Party.

Strict security surrounded the visit to Halton House, near Wendover, in December 1977 of the Prime Minister, Mr James Callaghan and President Giscard de'Estaing of France. Held in what was more normally used as the Officers Mess for RAF Halton – a former Rothschild mansion – the press conference was attended by reporters, photographers and TV crews from around the world and followed talks between the two leaders at nearby Chequers.

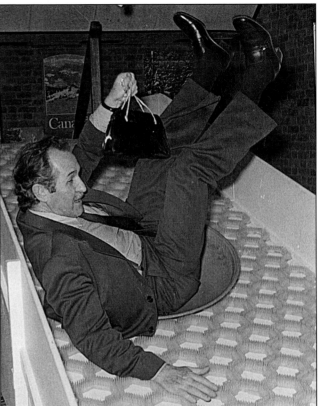

Oops! There can be a lighter side to local politics as Doug Joss, secretary to the chairman of Aylesbury Vale District Council, discovered (*top right*) when he accompanied her to the opening of a week long exhibition on Canada staged at the Civic Centre in March 1979. The exhibition, described as being the largest event of its kind ever to take place in a provincial town, had been organised by the local education committee and the Commonwealth Institute for the benefit of local schools. Why is he holding a handbag? It belonged to the chairman, Councillor Mrs Edna Embleton who tried the mini ski slope with more success (*top left*) and who is seen (*bottom*) offering some headwear advice to district secretary Graham Worrall.

They don't make them like Jessie any more. With a smile and a wave for our camera, Jessie Steward set off from her Cheddington home in May 1979 to vote in the general election – on the day that she celebrated her 105th birthday. Admitting to being a lifelong Tory, she had gone to the polls in every general election since women gained the right to vote. Members of the village Conservative Association gave her a surprise birthday party, but only after she had cast her vote.

Paraplegics in the famous spinal injuries wards at Stoke Mandeville Hospital were able to claim a resounding victory in November 1979 after the Minister of State for Health, Dr Gerard Vaughan, who visited them, assured them that one of the wards – Ward 5 – would not be closing. As a cost cutting exercise the Bucks Area Health Authority had planned to shut the 31-bed ward but had put making a decision on hold until after the Minister's visit.

SPORT FOR ALL

For the first time Aylesbury District League Premier Division side Stone United (*top*) became holders of the top trophy to be played for in local football – the Field Shield – by easily defeating Bierton, 3-0, in April 1972. Bierton had won the shield on seven previous occasions. And in the same month and year it was a hard fought game in the Oving Villages Cup Final when Aston Clinton (*bottom*) held off Haddenham with a score of 1-0.

Aylesbury carried off the Bucks Cup with a resounding 7-0 victory over Marlow when they played at Weston Turville in February 1974. It was the fourth time in five years that Aylesbury had won the competition.

Penalty area action from the Amateur Cup game played at Victoria Park, Aylesbury in September 1973 when Aylesbury United 'with cool efficiency', drove off a challenge from Hazells, 4-0.

This action shot comes from the Field Shield match which took place at Hazells sports ground, Aylesbury, in 1978.

Sport for all! This was the scene following the Aylesbury Middle Schools Cup Final held at Broughton School in May 1975. The game was between Haydon County Middle School and Oak Green County Middle, with both teams having something to celebrate after the match… it was a draw.

The deputy mayor of Aylesbury, Ald Horace Poole, officially opened the Aylesbury Rugby Football Club ground at Ostlers Field, Weston Turville in October 1970, the ground having been named after club chairman Mr Ron Ostler. As part of the celebrations a game was played between Aylesbury and the Bucks County XV, the latter winning 41-14.

A group of veterans from Aylesbury Rugby Football Club – the over 35s – went on their first trip overseas, as a team, in November 1979 and visited Aarhus in Denmark. They played one fixture and lost 20-0!

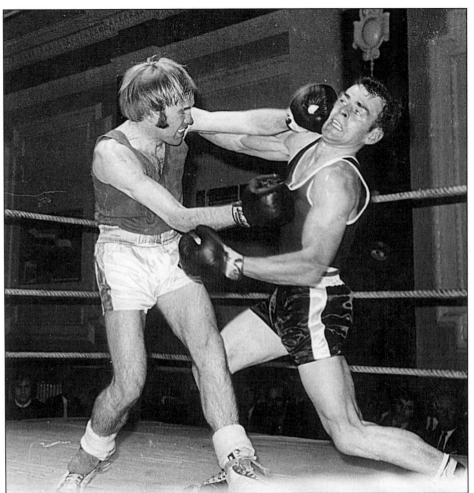

Aylesbury featherweight Ron Hewitt is seen here in action at the Borough Assembly Hall in the town in November 1971 in a tournament where he met and defeated J. Murphy from the Blackbird Leys Club to win the challenge trophy sponsored by local car dealership Perrys.

Trophies, including one to local heavyweight Mick Hoyland, were presented by Jimmie Ellis, police sergeant Bert Lynch in the popular BBC TV series *Z Cars* and Robert Fielding (alias PC Quilley), following a boxing tournament held at the Aylesbury Borough Assembly Hall in November 1971.

Professional middleweight boxer Oscar Angus (*right*) from Aylesbury produced one of his best performances to date when, in March 1976, he came up against Kevin Finnegan, the former British and European middleweight champion at the Anglo-American Sporting Club, London. 'Although Angus lost on a decisive points margin, his performance was full of tenacity and courage', we reported.

Aylesbury Grammar School hero Mark Rose (17) is hoisted aloft by school friends as they congratulate him on his selection in March 1979, to the England rugby under-19's side for their forthcoming matches against Scotland, France and Wales.

Exhibition bouts by members of the Aylesbury Boxing Club were among the attractions at the Hazells Club fete held at the sports ground off Oakfield Road, Aylesbury in August 1979.

'Our Enery', boxer Henry Cooper, popped in to the Stocklake Sports and Social Club, Aylesbury, on 8 November 1979 to present awards to those who had taken part in the first marathon race to be organised by the Aylesbury Canoe Club.

It was gruelling, but every year there was a good turnout for the annual Coombe Hill race at Wendover, and 1977 was no exception. A total of 99 runners finished the race, organised by the Wendover Carnival Committee, a number of them raising money for local charity. The race took them from the centre of the village to the top of nearby Coombe Hill – a hill from which, it is said, on a clear day you can see seven counties – and back again.

With so many changes taking place in and around the Aylesbury area, many were beginning to think it was something of a topsy-turvey world. And as if to prove the point, members of the Aylesbury Gymnastics Club gave this rather unusual display to welcome in the new decade.

Hurdler Richard Andrews (*right*) and high jumper Keith Ramsden (*bottom*) caught in action during a practice training session for the Aylesbury Athletics Club at the Edinburgh Playing Fields, Aylesbury, in August 1970. 'Vale AC are now involved in league athletics, the latest development in the sport which will mean increased activity for club members', we reported.

It certainly was no fisherman's tale. This giant cat fish was caught, believe it or not, at the Wilstone reservoir close to Aylesbury in 1970, mounted and then presented to the Tring Museum for safe keeping – and to make sure that when the story of its capture was told, those in doubt could call in and see it for themselves.

This photograph was taken in June 1975 to celebrate the 50 years that Harry Ridgeway of Aylesbury – and president of the Aylesbury Invitation Flying Club – had kept pigeons, his first being one given to him at the age of 14 by his father. 'Pigeons will always be in my blood', Harry told our reporter who, like our photographer was a little surprised when they turned up at his home after accepting the invitation to meet him from the Invitation Flying Club. 'We took it to literally mean something to do with flying, like planes, and thought there might be a flight in it for us. But no matter, it was a lovely local story', he said.

Thank goodness! More than 20 players from the Aylesbury Netball League breathed a sigh of relief as a fund raising 24-hour netball marathon came to an end in May 1975. But their efforts were well worth it, raising £700 towards the cost of a minibus for the Manor House Hospital in Aylesbury.

It was there for both sport and recreation – a great combination. This was the scene at the open-air swimming pool in the Vale Park in centre of Aylesbury in August 1974, a pool which has since been filled in and replaced by a modern swimming and fitness centre, the Aqua Vale.

It is never too early to start discovering the pleasure that competition sport can provide as the youngsters in these delightful pictures obviously found out during the annual sports day held at Bedgrove School, Aylesbury, in June 1972.

Determination, effort and sheer pluck. That's what these youngsters from Oak Green School in Aylesbury were showing during this track event at their annual sports day held in June 1972 – cheered on, of course, by their school chums.

CUSTOMS AND CRAFTS

Go for it girls! The picture shows competitors in a pancake race held in the Friars Square shopping centre in 1973 who were raising money for the charity Shelter. This was the early 1970s version of the shopping centre which, at the time, had one of the largest Woolworth stores in Europe.

It might be a case of trial and error but these youngsters from Haddenham were certainly making the effort at tossing their pancakes when they took part in the traditional pancake race in the village in 1973.

In the sweltering heat of the summer of 1976, Morris Men from as far afield as Leicester and Derby turned up in Market Square, Aylesbury to take part in what was to be a prelude to the Whitchurch Morris Men's annual day of dance and feast which was held at Wilstone. Some found the going just too hot (*above*) and were quite happy to have their brows mopped by some of those who had watched their performance – no doubt waiting as well, with tankards strapped to their belts, as many Morris Men have, to pop into the nearest local hostelry for a refreshing pint. And while that was going on the Morris Men's Squire had a chance to meet some of the crowd including young Matthew Ford (*below*).

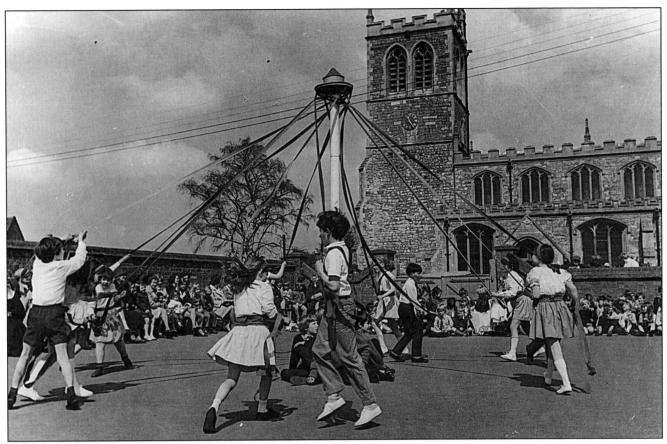

The traditional May Pole dance – this picture was taken at Wingrave in 1971.

A custom in Bucks and around the Aylesbury area was traditionally the regular 'meets' of the hunt and this picture was taken in December 1972 at Winslow.

Always part of Christmas – the choir singing at St Mary's Parish Church, Aylesbury, in 1972.

It is a ceremony which dates back to the 17th century – the Beating of the Bounds. And in the parish of Waddesdon they take this very seriously, performing the ancient rite every seven years, the most recent being in 2002, with villagers spending two days walking, no matter what the weather, their parish boundary. And there are ceremonies en-route such as making crosses on trees or the ground where the parish boundary ends and, for some of the younger people taking part, an initiation by being given 'the bumps' or even having themselves lifted aloft, turned over and patted 'on the rump' with a shovel. Quirky, but quaint... long may it continue.

On parade. These were the scenes in Market Square, Aylesbury, in April 1971 as Scouts, Cubs, Guides and Brownies gathered to mark St George's Day.

What a smart turn out. These youngsters (*top*) are pictured on their way to St Mary's Parish Church, Aylesbury, in April 1972 for a special service, which followed a parade through the town, to mark St George's Day. Local dignitaries were among those who joined in the service including on this occasion (*bottom*) the Mayor of Aylesbury, Councillor Mrs Zena Williams.

St George's Day was, for many years, celebrated in Aylesbury with a procession through the town centre. Here are more pictures of what it was like as the parade took place in 1972… do you, we wonder, recognise anyone in these photographs from 30 years ago?

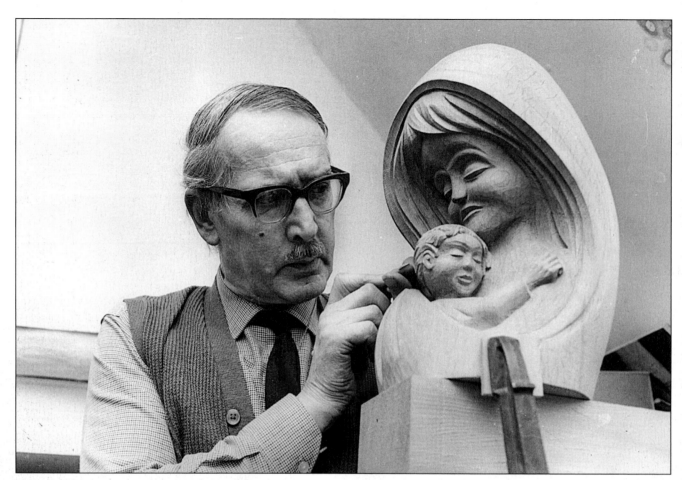

They are studies in perfection. The skills involved with woodcarving and the making of stained glass windows are summed up in these two pictures taken of local craftsmen in the 1970s.

For nearly 50 years Walter Small had the job he loved – making and repairing shoes at St John's Hospital at Stone. He retired in 1976 and recalled the days when he served his apprenticeship with a cobbler in Aylesbury and also worked, for a time, for the ill-fated Cubitts motor car company in Aylesbury which went bankrupt in 1925. 'If I had my way I would go on working for ever, but they won't let you nowadays', he said.